W9-BHE-747

THE BIG SNOW

By Howard Gutner

Illustrated by Marisol Sarrazin

Modern Curriculum Press
Parsippany, New Jersey

Computer colorizations by Lucie Maragni

Book design by Denise Ingrassia

Modern Curriculum Press
An imprint of Pearson Learning
299 Jefferson Road, P.O. Box 480
Parsippany, NJ 07054–0480

www.pearsonlearning.com

1-800-321-3106

© 2000 Modern Curriculum Press, an imprint of Pearson Learning, a division of Pearson Education Inc. All rights reserved. Printed in the United States of America. This publication is protected by Copyright and permissions should be obtained from the publisher prior to any prohibited reproduction, storage in a retrieval system, or transmission in any form or by any means, electronic, mechanical, photocopying, recording, or likewise. For information regarding permission(s), write to Rights and Permissions Department. This edition is published simultaneously in Canada by Pearson Education Canada.

ISBN 0-7652-1367-2

2 3 4 5 6 7 8 9 10 UP 08 07 06 05 04 03 02 01 00

**Modern
Curriculum
Press**

Contents

To all those who help
a friend or a neighbor in need

Chapter 1
The Big Surprise

"Zack! It's time to get up!"

Zack could hear his mother calling from the kitchen. He looked at the clock. It was already eight o'clock. He was going to be late for school!

Zack quickly got dressed. Then he ran into the kitchen. His mother was sitting at the table, listening to the radio.

"Mom, why didn't you wake me up?" Zack asked. "I'm going to be late for school."

Mom smiled. Then she laughed. "Look outside, Zack," she said.

Zack walked over to the window. His eyes got very big. "Wow!" he said. "When did it start to snow?"

"The snow started last night," Zack's mother said, "after you went to sleep."

8

Zack pressed his nose against the window. Outside, the snow covered everything. There were no cars. There were no bushes. Everything looked like big white marshmallows.

Zack listened to the radio.

"The biggest storm in thirty years has hit Lakeland. Most roads have not been cleared. All schools are closed," a man said.

"Hooray!" said Zack. "Can I go out and play in the snow?"

Zack's mother smiled. "You can go out after breakfast," she said.

Chapter 2
A Friend in Need

Zack put on his boots, mittens, a hat, and his warmest coat. With so much clothing on, he looked much bigger than he really was.

Zack's first step into the snow surprised him. The snow was almost up to his knees.

Zack's father had just finished shoveling the driveway. "Hey, Dad!" called Zack. "Let me help you shovel the walk."

"Thanks," Zack's dad said.

Zack shoveled the snow from the walk into a big pile. Then he climbed on top of the pile. He could see all of B Street. Snow covered the front steps of every house.

Zack saw his friend Lisa in her yard across the street. "Hi, Lisa!" Zack yelled, "Isn't all this snow great?"

"No!" Lisa yelled back. "It's awful. I can't find my cat, Snowball. I think she's outside somewhere."

"I'll help you look for her," said Zack.
He waded through the snow to Lisa's yard.

"Hey, Zack! Lisa!" two voices called.
"The snow is so much fun! Come on over!" Andy and Katy were trying to roll a big ball of snow across Andy's front yard.

"Not now!" yelled Zack. "We have a problem."

"I can't find Snowball," Lisa told them.

"Oh, no!" said Katy. "We'll come over and help you."

"How did Snowball get out?" asked Andy as he and Katy came into the yard.

Lisa said, "When I woke up, I opened a window to touch the snow. I closed it later. Then I couldn't find Snowball anywhere. I think she went out the window. I looked for prints outside, but the wind was blowing the snow around."

"Don't worry, Lisa," Andy said. "Cats are smart. Snowball is all right. We'll look for her."

Lisa looked around the street. "Everything is white. How will we ever see her? Snowball is white all over."

"We'll search the whole block," said Zack. "With four of us looking, we'll find Snowball."

Zack smiled as he talked, but he was worried. He didn't know how they would ever find a white cat in white snow.

Chapter 3
A Neighbor in Need

The B Street Kids went to tell their parents where they were going. Then they met back at Lisa's house.

"Let's go," said Andy.

"We've got another job to do, too," said Zack. "My mom told me that Mr. Martin called. He wants me to shovel his steps."

"I remember," said Katy. "Mr. Martin broke his leg last week. The snow must be a big problem for him."

"Let's go help him," said Zack.
He looked at Lisa. He could see she
was worried about Snowball.

"We can look for Snowball as we walk.
Then we can ask Mr. Martin if he has seen
Snowball," added Zack.

Zack, Katy, Andy, and Lisa walked to Mr. Martin's house. Mr. Martin opened the front door. "Am I glad to see you!" he said. "Don't walk up those steps. They might be slippery. I don't want any of you to fall."

"We'll clean off your steps," said Zack. The four kids started to shovel.

"Hold your shovel like this," said Katy. "The snow falls right off." Katy always thought of new ways to do things.

The four of them worked hard. At last, they were finished. Mr. Martin opened his front door again.

"Thank you!" he said. "Those steps are much safer now. I wish there was something I could do for you."

Lisa asked, "Have you seen my cat, Snowball? She's all white, just like the snow. She got out of the house."

"Oh, my!" said Mr. Martin. "It would be hard to find a white cat in the snow. I haven't seen her. I'll watch for her from my front window. I'll call you if I see her."

"Thank you," said Lisa sadly.

"Bye," said all the kids.

As they walked down the street, Lisa asked, "What can I do about Snowball?"

"I have an idea," said Zack. "We can go to the other houses on B Street to ask them if they have seen Snowball. We can also see if people need help with the snow."

"That's a great idea!" said Katy.
"Let's start with Mrs. Garcia," said Zack.

Chapter 4
The Search for Snowball

The kids walked down B Street. The snowplow had come down the street once. The wind had already blown a lot of snow back onto the street.

"I don't see anyone," Lisa said.

"The snow makes everything so quiet," Katy added. "It's like a big blanket."

They got to Mrs. Garcia's house. The
walk and the steps had been shoveled.

"It looks as if we're too late to help
shovel anything here," said Lisa.

"She may still need some help," said
Zack. "Let's go find out."

Katy, Zack, Lisa, and Andy walked up to Mrs. Garcia's front door. Zack rang the bell.

"Well hello, kids," said Mrs. Garcia. "What a nice surprise."

"We've been visiting people on B Street to see if they need help with the snow," said Zack.

"Is there anything we can do for you?" asked Katy.

"Maybe there is," said Mrs. Garcia. "I'll be right back."

When she came back to the door, her
two-year-old son followed her.

"Hi, Davey," the kids said. Davey smiled
back and giggled.

"What can we do to help?" asked Zack.

"I need some milk," said Mrs. Garcia. "Mr. Garcia is driving a big snowplow for the city. I can't leave Davey here alone, and the snow is too deep to take him outside."

"We can get milk for you," Andy said.

"Thanks. Are you having fun in all this snow?" Mrs. Garcia asked.

"Not really," Lisa said. "My cat is missing. Have you seen her?"

"No, I haven't been outside," said Mrs. Garcia. "Maybe Mr. Bailey at the store could help. He has a cat."

"That's right," said Zack. "He knows what cats do. Let's go!"

Chapter 5
A Clue

The B Street Kids left their shovels at Mrs. Garcia's house. Then they walked to the end of B Street to Mr. Bailey's store. A big gray cat sat near one of the windows.

"Look at that cat," Lisa said. "He doesn't want to go outside in the snow."

The kids went inside. "Hi, Mr. Bailey,"
they called.

"Hi, kids," said Mr. Bailey. "I heard you
have no school today. What have you been
doing?"

Zack said, "We've been helping people.
We need to get some milk for Mrs. Garcia."

Mr. Bailey smiled. "The milk is in the
back." He pointed to a glass door.

"We also hoped you could help us," said
Zack as Andy went to get the milk.

"Sure," said Mr. Bailey.

"I can't find my cat, Snowball," Lisa said. "I think she went out a window. I wish she just sat in the window like your cat does."

"Duffy doesn't always sit there," said Mr. Bailey. "Sometimes he runs out the door when people come in."

"What do you do then?" asked Zack.

Mr. Bailey said, "Duffy comes back in when another person opens the door. Sometimes I don't even see him come in."

"Maybe Snowball found a way to get back inside your house, Lisa," said Andy. He handed the milk to Mr. Bailey.

"I didn't think of that!" said Lisa.

"Let's go to your house and look," Katy said to Lisa.

Chapter 6

Snowball!

Andy, Katy, Zack, and Lisa hurried up B Street as fast as they could. When they got to Mrs. Garcia's house, Zack ran to the front door. He gave Mrs. Garcia the milk, got the shovels, and ran back.

When Lisa opened her front door she called, "Mom, Mom! Has Snowball come home?"

"No, I haven't seen her," her mom called from the kitchen.

As the kids came into the kitchen, they saw that Lisa's mom was fanning herself. "Mom," Lisa said, "why are you so warm? It's cold outside!"

"I was doing the laundry downstairs," said Lisa's mom. "It got so hot that I opened the window. When I went back downstairs, I saw that the snow had blown in through the window. So I just closed it."

Zack's eyes popped open. He said, "I know where Snowball is! Lisa, think about what your mom just said."

"Ummm," Lisa thought. Then she smiled. "You're right."

"Why don't we check in the basement?" said Zack.

Downstairs, the kids started to look around. Zack looked by the window.

"Lisa!" Zack cried. He pointed to a laundry basket. It was filled with fluffy, white towels. Snowball was sleeping right on top of the towels.

"Snowball!" Lisa called.

"Meow," Snowball said. Lisa picked her up and hugged her.

"She must have come in through the window when your mom left it open," Zack said. "When she went to sleep on the towels, your mom didn't see her because both the towels and the cat are white."

"Now that we've found the cat, let's go outside and have some fun," Andy said. All the kids cheered.

As they went back upstairs, Katy said,
"Let's make a snow cat."

Everyone went to work rolling big
snowballs. When they finished, Zack patted
the snow cat's head.

"This is one cat that likes being outside
in the snow," he laughed.

Glossary

awful [AW ful] very bad

fanning [FAN nihng] making air move to cool someone or something

giggled [GIH guld] laughed with high, quick sounds

laundry [LAWN dree] clothes that need to be cleaned

prints [prihnts] marks made by an animal's foot

shovel [SHUH vul] tool with a long handle, used for digging and lifting dirt and snow; or to dig using a shovel

slippery [SLIH puh ree] can cause you to slip and fall down

waded [WAYD ihd] walked slowly through water, mud, or snow